Cinderella

Key sound ow spellings: ow, ou
Secondary sounds: th, ll, wh

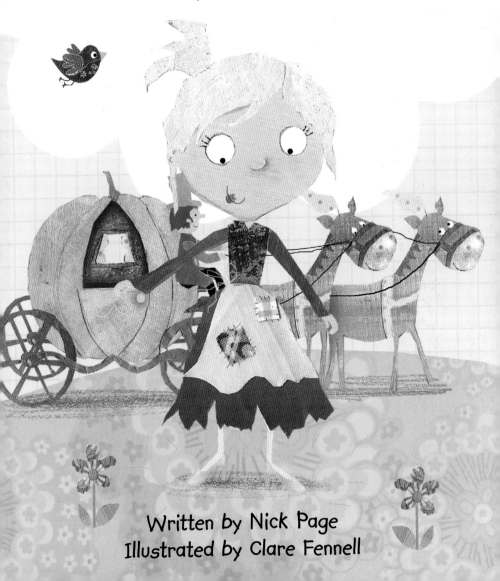

Written by Nick Page
Illustrated by Clare Fennell

"Cinderella, clean the house!"
"Cinderella, wash my blouse!"
"Cinderella, you behave!"
"Cinderella, you're a slave!"
Every day, they'd howl and shout
and order the poor girl about.

The magic wand spins round and round.
Will Cinderella's prince be found?

Wicked stepmom
makes her clean,

two stepsisters are so mean.

6

Not allowed a nice, warm bed,
she sleeps by the fire instead,
near the ashes, in the cellar,
so they call her Cinderella.

The magic wand spins round and round.
Will Cinderella's prince be found?

An announcement to the town:
"Every girl, put on your gown,
it's the party of your life!
The prince is scouting for a wife!"
"What shall I wear?" Cinders asks.
"You can't go! Back to your tasks!"

The magic wand spins round and round.
Will Cinderella's prince be found?

As the others head to town,
Cinders cries. She's feeling down.

When – POW! – a fairy dame appears.
"You shall go to the ball, my dear!
Your fairy godmother has arrived –
now dry your eyes and get outside."

The magic wand spins round and round.
Will Cinderella's prince be found?

11

She waves her wand – round and round,
and Cinders has a lovely gown,
a magic carriage made of gold,
and two glass shoes (they're very cold).

"Be home before
the midnight hour,
or else this spell
will lose its power."

The magic wand spins round and round.
Will Cinderella's prince be found?

13

Dong! Dong! Dong!

At the ball, the crowd's amazed,
the prince is wowed – completely dazed.
And all that night, this charming fella
dances just with Cinderella.
Until the clock bells in the tower
start to chime the midnight hour!
The magic wand spins round and round.
Will Cinderella's prince be found?

"It's midnight now! I must get out!
I've got to go! Can't wait about!"
And as the spell starts losing power,
she runs at ninety miles an hour!

On the steps, she leaves behind
a glass shoe for the prince to find.

The magic wand spins
round and round.
Will Cinderella's
prince be found?

Around the town Prince Charming goes,
fitting the glass shoe on the toes
of every girl, even her sisters.
(They vow it fits, despite the blisters.)

"Try me!" A sound comes from the cellar.
"Pipe down," shouts Mom to Cinderella.

Try me!

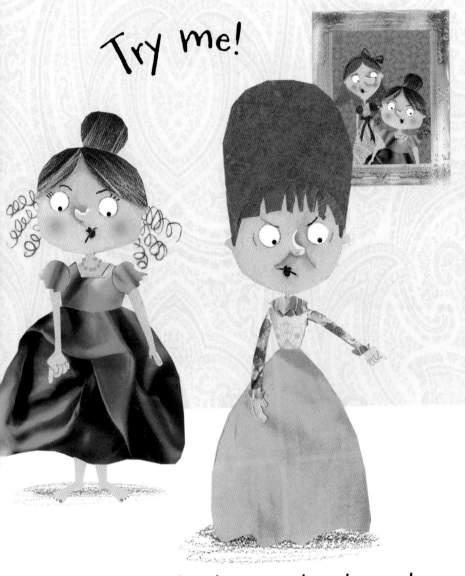

The magic wand spins round and round.
Will Cinderella's prince be found?

"You know you're not allowed upstairs!"
"No! Bring her out!" the prince declares.
The glass shoe fits her perfectly.
Her stepmom cries, "It cannot be!"
But Cinders has the other shoe!
The prince says,
"Take a bow – it's you!"

Perfect!

The magic wand spins round and round.
Will Cinderella's prince be found?

Bells are ringing – hear the sound
of happy endings all around.
Cinders and the prince are wed;
he sets a crown upon her head.
Everyone is so delighted!
(But not Stepmom – she's not invited!)

The magic wand spins round and round.
Cinderella's prince is found!

Key sound

There are different groups of letters that make the **ow** sound. Practice them by looking at the words in Cinderella's gowns and using them to make sentences. Can you use each word in a different sentence?

house

blouse

about

shout

sound

around

outside

announce

clown

frown

crown

town

gown

crowd

allowed

tower

power

Letters together

Look at these pairs of letters and say the sounds they make.

th   **ll**   **wh**

Follow the words that contain th to help Cinderella find her godmother.

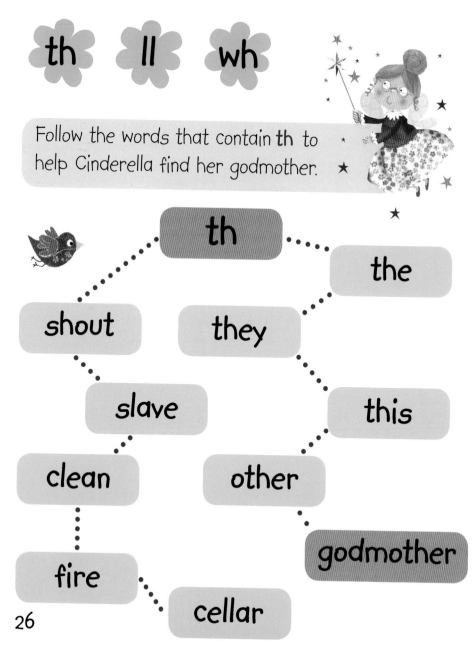

th

the

shout

they

slave

this

clean

other

fire

godmother

cellar

Follow the words that contain **ll** to ring the wedding bells for Cinderella.

ll

cellar

shoe

crown

prince

spell

wife

party

bells

lots .... other

Follow the words that contain **wh** to help Cinderella find her white dress.

what

wh

when

why

slipper

other

clean

white

where

Rhyming words

Read the words in the flowers and point to other words that rhyme with them.

prince   **gown**   down

shoes   crown

clean   shock

clock

knock   dance

house   tell

spell

fell   blouse

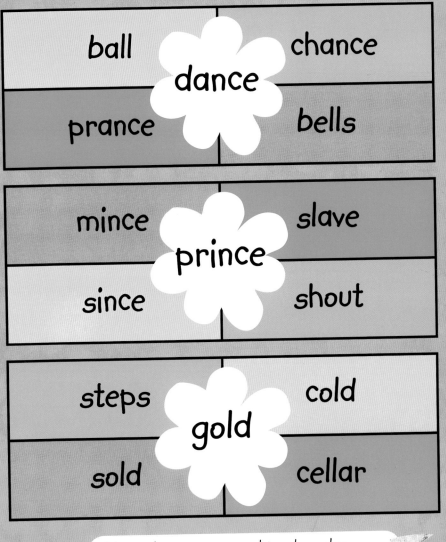

ball   dance   chance

prance   bells

mince   prince   slave

since   shout

steps   gold   cold

sold   cellar

Now choose a word and make up a rhyming chant!

I wear a **crown** and a **gown** as I spin **round** and **round**.

29

Sight words

Many common words can be difficult to sound out. Practice them by reading these sentences about the story. Now make more sentences using other sight words from around the border.

Cinderella and the prince danced **and** danced.

The prince tried the shoe on **every** girl.

The fairy **made** shoes and a gown for Cinderella.

Cinderella went **to** the ball.

There was an invitation **from** the prince!

to • there's • every • cold • ever • across • from • as